One O One
For Everyone

Learn & Earn

Creative Imitation

Gabriel Sinki

ISBN-13: 978-1463610814
ISBN-10: 1463610815

DEDICATION

For the entrepreneurs who are working hard to create jobs and to improve our quality of life. To make products and services available at better quality, easier to use, with added value at affordable prices.

CONTENTS

Tools of creative imitators, or weapons for fending competitors:

1. Fix the Problem;
2. Leaders in Me-Too;
     - Migrators
     - Industrial or home services
     - Taste
3. Self Competing; (Only to protect your position)
4. Make it same or better for less;
5. Upscale it.

ACKNOWLEDGMENTS

Thanks to James McCurley for his English editing.
Special Thanks to Stephanie Rabbat for her inputs of ideas and editing work

"If You Are Building A Car To Take On The Legendary High-Performance Sedans, Just Making It Equal Means You Have Failed."

A Lexus Advertisement

"Once upon a time a carpenter had a monkey for a pet. This monkey was the master of "monkey see monkey do." It watched his master working on sowing a large wooden plank. The monkey watched and watched but finally the temptation of "Me -Too" became irresistible. At the first occasion when he was left alone to his own devices, he jumped on the plank and started sawing. It was not long before his tail got caught into the split of the plank"

And so it goes that many uncreative "ME-TOO" imitators got their tail caught.

The urge to imitate is not only practiced by the small entrepreneur, it is also a phenomenon that persists with large corporations. Statistics provide the proof that truly innovative products in the marketplace - that are not based on slight variations of existing products are below

8%. (Source MIS, for the year 1995) My observation from working with large corporations is that many of them wanted to be like the competitor, while their competitor wanted to be like them. This fact was confirmed in an article entitled Nextel Chases Teens: "Nearly every U.S. cellular carrier these days wants to be more like Nextel Communications, Inc. Ironically, Nextel seems to want to be something else" (WSJ 04/13.04).

It is often said that we live in a world of "ME-TOO." Just look around you and you will see that imitators are all over the map. Cars are getting so similar in shape that one has difficulty recognizing their make. In the 90's consumers had difficulty differentiating between Chevrolet and Pontiac or Buick and an Oldsmobile. In this case "we met the imitator's and it is us. You need only to take a short trip to your local grocer to experience this first hand. Grocery store shelves are filled with so many "Me-Too" products; raising the question of what is the difference between all these similar products.

Sometimes unfair imitation could ruin business for a whole market. The Japanese, before they gained their recent industrious wisdom, were major copycats. For decades their national growth was no cause for celebration.

On the other hand if an imitator is creative enough he can displace the number one producer from its position. Al Ries & Jack Trout in their two books: Positioning; The Battle for Your Mind; and the 22

Immutable laws of Marketing, stress the fact that to be first in the market place with a good product, guarantees a number one position. This is very true until a creative imitator succeeds to displace the original innovator and becomes number one. A case in point would be the story of Lego. If you asked in the year 2000 who was the first in "Children's' Building Blocks" Lego would be the answer. But the imitator "Mega Bloks" was in black while Lego had a loss of more than $150 million in.

More examples of losing leadership position:

❖ Frigidaire, the original leader and first in the home refrigerator business, lost their leading share position

❖ Cadillac no longer holds the number one position in luxury cars being displaced by BMW, Lexus,

❖ IBM is no longer the leader in the personal computers business, as a result of strong competitors like Apple

❖ Prodigy in 1992 with 860,000 members had the leadership position compared to AOL with 181,000 members. Where is Prodigy today?

❖ Where are the 1997 sixdegress.com, the 2002 Friendster and the bunch of dozens or so of me-too social networking compared to today 2006 Face Book and Twitter?

❖ What is the market share of Blackberry compared to that of iPad in 2011?

The imitator would have never shaken the leadership position of the original if the act of duplication were just a Me-Too type. But many number one positions got displaced because of Creative imitators. They just added one or more attributes to the existing product. This is not much different from the antiquity entrepreneur who claimed: "you find something people want, and you bring it out better and cheaper than the next man." But today's entrepreneurs have more tools to add to this old adage.

Copyright and patent protection:

Copycats and knock-off products are not only for the simple innovations. Semiconductors, computers and software are being copied in spite of the seemingly protective patents and copyrights. Even the best-written patents limits exact "knock-off" only, but allow developers who make similar but potentially valuable complementary changes to the product. In an article entitled "Brothers of Innovations" published by the Wall Street Journal on April 19, 2004 the question of patent protection is discussed. It quotes Mr. James O'Shaughnessy, Vice President and chief intellectual property counsel at Rockwell Automation Inc. in Milwaukee: "We design around competitor patents on a regular basis, ---to produce an equivalent product that doesn't infringe." The article recounts other stories of how patents owners lost protection, when they solely depended on it. Patent owners should thus look for added marketing pre-emptive protections.

The tools discussed in here, do not only address those who are on the outside but also those who should protect their products from outsiders. It particularly addresses those who have a high market share of a product and leave it vulnerable to competitive attacks. The wisdom is to remember that it is quite a task to reach a successful position in the market place, but it is more of a daunting job to keep that position. Successful entrepreneurs have always put themselves on the other side of the fence. They look at their product from an outsider's unbiased view and try to imagine what a competitor would do to snatch a portion of their market share. They stayed ahead of the game by applying well-studied and tested improvement. They never believed in the dictum: if isn't broke don't fix it. Is there a better example of what happening to the wireless phone of the year 2011? What more improvement and applications, as an example, can be added to an "iphone 5". In general consumer is wondering is it a phone, a camera, a GPS, etc.

In all the cases when leadership was lost or a market share was sliced by competitors, it was the entrepreneurial spirit that applied the Drucker's principle of **"hit them were they ain't."** For many products they lack one thing or another. This is due to:

- ❖ Development under a culture of "I would rather be in the market place first with a product of average quality, than be there late with a perfect product."
- ❖ At the time of its launching the technology to make it better was not available;
- ❖ Product launch not being wholly customer oriented;
- ❖ Consumer's needs, taste, like and dislike change.

Tools of creative imitators, or weapons for fending competitors:

6. Fix the Problem;
7. Leaders in Me-Too;
   - Migrators
   - Industrial or home services
   - Taste
8. Self Competing; (Only to protect your position)
9. Make it same or better for less;
10. Upscale it.

Fix the Problem:

How would you like to fix a problem and receive $3 billion or more in compensation for your services. In late April 2004 the media was fixated on this story. It is the story of Larry Page and Sergey Brin the founders of Google and their IPO which was to be launched soon. It all started with the lousy search engines that answered all the questions except for the one you asked for. Page and Brin, two former Stanford computer-science students, took advantage of the problem of inaccuracy of search engines, and turned it into an excellent search quest that most users and internet providers actually use. They simply reinvented the search, to be focused and accurate. Everyone knew that the search engines of that time needed to be fixed, but only Page and Brin solved it.

But in other instances the defect is not so obvious. T. Dillon advises that in this case, one has to probe the real consumer mind. For if you ask the consumer simply what they want, they will repeat what they hear in the media: Low fat, healthy food, better service, convenience etc. Rather, he advises to probe the consumer's mind to complain (which is the one universal talent among human beings,) and you will get a totally different direction.

The key then is to find out what is lacking, in need of correction or improvement. Once the imitator or the product's owner finds out what the real bug in the product or service is, he will be on the right track. A good example is the story of Best Food's entry into the crowded gravy market. Best Food, in the mid 1980's, must have probed the consumer's mind for complaints about existing gravy products. Consumers clearly indicated the nuisance and time consuming problem dealing with lumpy gravies. Best Food came up with a new product highlighting the resolved problem: "ANNOUNCING THE END OF LUMPY GRAVY." It was an instant thickener with instant success.

In the early 2000's some of the outfits of the online suit-sellers asked consumers what improvements they should undertake; the response has been safeguard of the credit card, faster delivery and the usual jargons. But when the probing question was asked, the answer was the problem of trying the cloth. In response, some online stores tried new pitch: Fetch it yourself. Retailers urge Internet shoppers to pick up purchases in person; making sure the shoe fits." Others make return goods easier by allowing online customers to return the unwanted purchases to store locations near them. For the question of online theft, Citigroup pioneered the idea to provide their customer with credit cards that generate random numbers. In general, the number can be used for one single purchase only.

In other cases, problems that needed to be fixed were obvious to both consumers and producers but the technology was not yet available to solve it. There are Entrepreneurs who are vigilant about advances in technology and seize every opportunity to fix the problem. As a result, they usually slice a good market share for themselves. The following are some examples:

- In the early 2000's, Using new technology, cell phones were enabled to function nationally and internationally in many areas.
- Improving Internet calls by applying VOIP technology; hence the birth of Vonage, Nettalk, Magic Jack and all the other imitators.
- Digital cameras improvement in offering fast continuous shots.
- Car safety improvement such as rear view monitor, amongst many other feature developed and in the process of development.

All the above cases are just a small sample of changing problems into opportunities. Competition drives industries to continually improve their products, while increasing profits.

2- Leaders in Me-Too:

This is where one industry/service is copying idea(s) from another totally different industry. Although the concept might be copied exactly the same it is still a creative way to copy. As an example, historically auctions were used mainly to liquidate the spoils of wars and slaves. Someone applied the same tool to sell arts and real estates. These imitators are creative, because they were the first to copy an idea from one business to another. They took the chance to copy from unrelated industries or cultures.

2.1 - **Copying Habits From Other Cultures:**
"We came, we saw, we copied"

- Migration of food habits from one country to the other, this is well evidenced by the global growing of, chain and eclectic type restaurants.
- The East is copying the West, and vice versa in festivities such as Mother's and Father's day.

2.2 – **Copy Ideas From Other Industries Or Services**
In Mid April of 2004, the media and newspapers were laughing at Pfizer's latest consumer's offer: "Buy Six Viagra Prescriptions, The Seventh Is Free!" The Wall Street Journal claimed that the company tested the idea with patients and received overwhelming positive results. It all started with the low-end services and products such as buy one get one free. It then evolved into free mileage from cars, travel companies, and credit cards. In this case however, although it sounds funny, Pfizer marketer were pioneers in copying the idea from other industries.

Only a few days after Pfizer's Rx offer, Novartis announced that they will refund patients using Diovan or lotrel if their blood-pressure goal is not achieved. While issuing refunds is a common practice for department stores, this was a first for prescription drugs. Diovan is not small stuff, and according to NDC Health, Atlanta sales of the drug approached $1.5 Billion in 2004. What is noteworthy here is the fact that pharmaceutical companies have borrowed ideas from other industries.

Since the most familiar product to all of us is food, I will use food products as an example to illustrate. Restaurants used to just mimic home cooking. As dinning out has evolved, chefs have surpassed the simplicity of a home cooked meal. This opened the door to food processors to copy restaurants. In the early 1970s they started to hire Chefs to form new models and better tasting standards. Here are some examples of the industry copying fast foods restaurant:

- Hamburgers (similar to MacDonald or Burger King etc.) that can be stored frozen.
- Chicken nuggets imitating Mcnuggets. Later on, Green Giant offers Veggie Nuggets.
- Restaurant Soups (Campbell) and Restaurant Pies (Rttenhouse) offered in supermarkets.
- The success of cold Pasta salad of the 90s. were imitated by the food industry. (Green Giant's Pasta Accent and others)

- Gourmet, Ready to eat, Meals by Marie Callenders' advertised as "CANCEL YOUR DINNER RESERVATIONS."
- Fondue specialties are now made easier to offer at home, with ready to use sweet and savory fondue mixes.

2.3 - Copying Taste:

In addition to habits and ideas being mimicked, flavors too have been copied and used as flavoring for unlikely products. This is evident from desserts to breakfast foods:

- Confectionary copying from a salty food: Reese's copying the taste of peanut butter in their chocolate peanut cup.
- Cereals that carry the taste of Graham crackers, short cake cookies, French toast, popcorn, waffle and more are being introduced. Other examples of copying a popular taste from one industry to another are:

Ice cream industry copying the taste of confectionary, creating a whole line of frozen confectionary novelties: frozen candy ice cream bars such as three musketeers, Hendrie's crunchy hazelnut Nougles, Borden Cracker Jack (popcorn and peanuts) and many others made this category the second fastest growing novelty of ice cream in 1984.

- The popular taste of popcorn snack was copied onto the chicken popcorn.

3- **Copy yourself in self competing**:

Hoffman La Roche used to own a well-known perfume supply company, Roure, as a subsidiary. Few years later they acquired Givaudan and that also had a perfume supply division. The mother company, HLR, kept both companies separate and each totally working independently and honestly competing against each other. That was before the years of consolidation and merging subsidiaries for better efficiencies. Owning two companies, and allowing them to do the same thing and competing with one another, seemed at the time a means in which to slow down the competition. The Wall Street Journal reported (2004) that the Royal Bank is self-competing. Royal Bank of Scotland Group PLC owns two branches on the New Bridge Street, in London (NatWest and Royal Bank) where both branches, are engaged in a fierce competition. To quote the WSJ: "Apparently Royal Bank has bought myriad brands and left them to duke it out."

Major airlines will not quietly watch those low fare competitors just take away business from them. In self-competing acts Delta's offered discount fares thru its Song's discount arm.

4 – **Make It Same or Better For Less:**

Creative Imitations

Simply cost cutting to compete for the same market, service or product is non-creative and the success is usually short lived. For 30 years since the 1970s, many large corporations such as Sunbeam, AT&T and Ford Motor have tried simple non-creative cost cutting with unlucrative results. The nasty fight between Dell and HP that cut profits to almost nothing was a well-known flop. However, later on it seems that other corporations knew how to do it right. The ultimate in creative imitation would be to make your imitation copy **"Faster, Better, Smaller/Bigger For Less"**

Absolutely nothing beats the technology driven lower prices. This happened in the era of the Mid. 80s. - 90s, where it seemed that technology was offering the advantage of "faster, better, with more for less." Computer chips were doubling in power every few months, while the cost was split. In the late 1990s, the storage capacity of hard drives doubled every year with prices going down. Such great strides in technology and other breakthroughs resulted in today's affordable PC's that have more power than some of the mainframe types of the early 80's. Digital cameras and cellular phones are other outstanding examples of the lower cost driven technology.

Cell phones are getting less expensive (when you consider all the values and features added) and more powerful. Manufacturers have added on so many features that cell phones are no longer just for making and receiving calls. It has now morphed into an "all in one" device that serves as a music player, video recorder, internet, games, camera and more.

But technology is not the only driving force here. There are some entrepreneurs that can impact the world without high tech gadgets. What is their driving force? Business savvy. The story of "People's Express" is now a case study in business textbooks. People's Express dissolved but dozens of other airlines learned from the pioneer's mistakes: Jet Blue, Transat, and many others are still striving.

Clearly, the tool most utilized is offering consumers the same product or service, where quality is uncompromised, for less. Simply cutting cost as we all know is the most detrimental two edged weapon of competing as we see it in the war between long distance providers, car dealers, soft drink manufacturers (the Coke war), internet providers and many more. Reducing prices thru cutting profits is mostly a temporary solution. Lower prices for lower quality products are doomed to fail. Many entrepreneurs succeeded in introducing lower prices for knock off of famous perfumes, and No Name Foods, but the success was short lived. In the case of food, Supermarket brand names, prevailed. There will always be inimitable stories about David beating Goliath. The latest is the success of "Crazy Cola" in a small Siberian City that had more than a 45% share of cola sales in 2003. Such stories exemplify local situation or temporary fads fueling profit. The most successful but simple means of competing thru lower prices are warehouse type consumer's stores (Costco) as well as discount chain stores such as

Creative Imitations

Wall Mart. Using their combined purchase muscles; then passing some of the saving on to consumers.

Lowering prices can be the very effective, for commodities or when it is executed in a well-planed value added design. Lower energy prices, hopefully sometime in the future, will be one of the most important industrial revolutions. Its rippling effect will be of the magnitude of tidal waves. Its effect on the industry and the world economy will be far stronger than any invention we have witnessed yet.

It seems that the future is always wide open for offering the same or better at economical prices. Some examples are:

- Hearing aids on average cost more than $2,000.00; while some experts believe that available technology could bring the cost down considerably.
- Making fashionable cloth, less expensive by offering knockoffs at lower prices and faster before the high-end fashion get there. Elite fashion houses used to consider such "Cheap Chic" as small stuff. But the growing influence of retailers such as Inditex SA's Zara, Hennes & Mauritz AB's H&M and Wal-Mart Stores are taking shares away from the high-end designers. (Making Fashion Faster WSJ/02/24/04)

5- Upscale it:

Same or better for more money

Manufacturers don't have to compete solely on the low end; they can also make their copied version upscale. While it was still possible to buy a good refrigerator for $500 in 2002, the market share of high-end refrigerators that cost more than $2,000.00 a piece seriously grew in 2002. GE offered models that could cost upwards of $8,000. This is applicable in all industries, provided that the right background and image is there.

The Future

Sample of Ideas for brainstorming

In the above we analyzed the past to provide a window on to the future. Using the above templates it would be of help to see future trends. Here are some examples of evolutionary changes in the 21st century that are happening in some dynamic fields:

Publishing:

Digital tools made publishing **"faster, better for less."** Will the next generation mostly read electronically? This fact leads us to a serious question. How will the impact be on the future of books, paper industry, book stores (already suffering), publishers, and a lot of other related business?

Communications:

Satellite phone requires a clear line of sight to the sky to connect globally especially in deserted remote areas. Will future technology solve the disadvantages of delayed talk and the expensive satellite minutes? If this is achieved, we might predict that the satellite phone will prevail. Just consider the advantages:

- Create a contact to civilization from wilderness.

- Stay in touch, as in the case of military;

- It can provide backup communication in disasters when cellular towers or landlines might not be functional.

Will Satellite Internet make also inroads in the internet field?

Arts:

Borrowing ideas from other fields:

How to stand up in a crowd? Ryan McGuiness, the famous art star, beside his use of vivid colors, differentiated his work by:

- Copying from pop iconography and silk-screening.
- Copying from Graffiti, changing a negative image to a beautiful art.
- Copied from signs and transformed them into attractive shapes, thus declared by authorities as a leading pioneer of the new semiotics.

- What distinguish the art work of Romero Brito? I will let art connoisseur analyze this. But in my humble opinion he was inspired by stained glass type art. i.e. copied ideas from stained glass art.

- The Industrial Mass Production concept is copied in the production of art in the so called "assembly line" for producing multiple copies of same painting.

- Did you know that some famous painters never held a brush? In fashion you need a famous name that people buy for the fame of that name. Mr. Alexander Gorlizki copied the idea. His work has been displayed in some major museums and his paintings sell for up to $10,000. His paintings are executed by several artists who work for him. He claims he does not do any of the work.

Copying nature with a twist:

Although most art work is based on copying nature, Biomimicry (from bios, meaning life, and mimesis, meaning to imitate) has inspired artists to copy ideas directly from nature with a new twist.

Computer-Technology:

iPad maintains market superiority by constantly applying new technologies, for efficiency and user friendly software. Its strength is the huge (and still growing) catalog of third-party apps. This makes it useful in business meetings, watching movies, reading news, books and more,

Real Estate:

- The condominium idea for housing is copied to develop condo hotels, condo offices and industrial park condos.
- Hotels lately redesigned their lobbies to imitate the atmosphere of Starbuck and Panera Bread.

Sports and athletics:

The Harlem Globetrotters Created in 1926 for basket ball black athletes, were the first to introduce humor and acrobatic entertainment to otherwise a tense serious game. They succeeded enormously nationally and internationally. They were creative in copying ideas from other fields. It took several years for someone else to adapt the concept. Jackie Chan made his fame and fortune by **not** being a me-too of another martial art movie maker. He rather injected the same idea of transforming serious type movies to an entertainment acrobatic comedy. Chan's innovation, gained him a place on the Hong Kong Avenue of Stars and the Hollywood Walk of Fame.

Most comedies are very hard to draw a smile; here is an example of how to produce new innovative comedy movies. Will such a concept be applied for Broadway? How can you transform serious to entertaining?

Financial:

- Banks copying financial institutions by adding wealth management services.
- Financial institution copying banks.

Car Industry:

Borrowing software/hardware technology to produce cars that are computer enhanced in safety and driving ease. Backing up monitors and alerts, automatic parking, are some examples? Will the future innovations go as far as automatic cruising, where cars will be enabled to travel long distances guided by GPS and avoid accidents and road blockage? But no matter what will come next, green and renewable cheap fuel will be the real breakthrough.

****

The above brief examples demonstrate how to use the "creative imitation" templates in prediction of future trends. More examples would be better left to readers to apply them creatively on the field of their interest.

In conclusion, of all the tools we examined to produce creative imitations, none is more effective as that of welcoming a problem. In business, someone's problem is another entrepreneur's opportunity.

Creative Imitations

ABOUT THE AUTHOR

Gabriel Sinki retired from a multinational company as vice president of its International Business Unit. He authored several papers on marketing and management. He conducted seminars for more than 20 years entitled "Innovations & Trends." This is the first template of several to follow.